KINGDOM MERCY

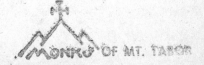

KINGDOM MERCY

*Living in the Power
of Forgiveness*

John Wimber

VINE
BOOKS

Servant Publications
Ann Arbor, Michigan

This edition copyright © 1987 by John Wimber

Cover design by Charles Piccirilli
Cover photo-illustration with sand by Lawrence Fitton

Vine Books is an imprint of Servant Publications
especially designed to serve Evangelical Protestants.

Published by Servant Books
P.O. Box 8617
Ann Arbor, Michigan 48107

90 91   10 9 8 7 6 5 4

Printed in the United States of America
ISBN 0-89283-360-2

KINGDOM MERCY

I learned a big lesson about forgiveness a few years back when I got involved in trying to help a young man who had recently come to the Lord (let's call him Jack). Jack's past life hadn't been too savory. In fact, he'd had a long history of trouble with the police and was still on probation from a previous offense when he got converted and started coming to our church.

He was one of those glorious cases that come along every so often—a person with a messed-up life and a seemingly endless list of things to repent of, who really goes all the way and gets utterly converted to Christ. We spent a lot of time together, talking about how Jesus could get him straightened around. It was a joy to watch Jack's life change right before my eyes.

Jack's one continuing problem was that he seemed either unable or unwilling to keep his meetings with his probation officer. It wasn't that he was rebellious or antagonistic toward his parole officer. He just hadn't learned to keep his priorities and responsibilities straight, and probation meetings were one of the things that just seemed to "fall through the cracks." He had been warned several times that he was going to be in trouble if he didn't hold up his end of the probation arrangement, and it was one of the things about which I tried hardest to encourage him.

Finally it happened. Jack had missed several meetings, and his probation officer had finally gotten fed up and put out a warrant for his arrest. I got called down to the police station to bail him out.

As I drove along, the whole thing made me feel sick. So many things had been going so well for Jack, and now *this*. Of course, taken by itself, missing a few meetings didn't seem all that awful. The problem, as Jack and I both knew very well, was that the judge wouldn't be taking it "by itself." Jack had a chronic problem with violating the terms of his probation, and the penalty for that could be severe. After all he had been through and all the progress he had made, this one problem could cost him a year in jail.

By the time I got to the police station I wasn't exactly in a cheery mood.

"Jack, why did you have to go and get yourself into this mess?" I snapped at him.

He just mumbled and turned his head away in shame. I guess it was an unfair question to ask him, anyway. What was he going to say to me? He obviously didn't go out and blow his probation because he *wanted* to get arrested and thrown in jail. He was miserable about his stumble, and so was I.

The night before the trial, I couldn't sleep. The lawyer hadn't held out much hope. "It's pretty open-and-shut," he had told me. I knew he was right. Jack's guilt was obvious, and the penalty was clearly spelled out in the law.

What still tormented me more than anything was the sheer stupidity of what Jack had done. He *knew* what he was supposed to do. He *knew* that if he didn't do it, he'd be found out. He *knew* what the penalty would be when he was. But he had gone right out and blown it anyway.

As I lay awake in bed, I prayed every way I could think to pray: for Jack, for the judge, against the judge, for wisdom for Jack's attorney, for *anything*. I recited every Scripture promise I could think of that seemed relevant.

Finally, in the midst of my tossings and turnings and wailings and moanings, the Lord managed to get a word in edgewise. "John," he seemed to whisper in my ear, "why don't you just ask me for *mercy?*"

That sounded pretty good. "Mercy, Lord," I prayed eagerly. "Mercy. Grant us your mercy. Be merciful to your son Jack. Mercy, Lord. Mercy. *Mercy. . . .*"

Then I dropped off to sleep.

The next day, in the courtroom, Jack still seemed to be in a daze, as if he weren't entirely aware of what was going on around him. Maybe he was trying to block it out, maybe he was just plain out of it. Frankly, having slept only a couple of hours the night before, I wasn't in much better shape myself.

After a while Jack's case was announced, and we went forward to stand before the judge. The judge sat there for a long time, shuffling through the papers in Jack's file, frowning down at us, then across at the clerk, then back at us. He seemed angry as he read and re-read the details of Jack's situation.

"Young man . . ." he said, peering down over the front edge of his desk, "Young man, this is . . . well, this is just plain *stupid*."

"I know how you feel," I thought to myself.

"Don't you realize you could get a year in prison for this?" the judge asked.

Jack just stared down at his shoes. He didn't say anything.

The judge sighed and slumped back in his chair. He didn't seem to be eager to say what he knew he had to say next.

Mercy, Lord, I prayed silently. *Mercy. . . .*

Suddenly the judge straightened up in his chair, stuffed all the papers back into the folder with Jack's name on it, and tossed it to the clerk, saying, "Case dismissed. Get him out of here."

Case dismissed! I couldn't believe my ears!

Neither, apparently, could Jack. He just kept standing there, staring down at the ground.

After a few moments the judge, who already had the papers for the next case spread out before him, noticed Jack still standing there. At first his eyes showed a flash of irritation. Then his expression softened.

"Young man," he said gently to Jack, "didn't you hear what I said?

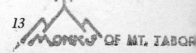

MONKS OF MT. TABOR

I've dismissed the charges against you. You can go. *You're free.*"

The Promise of Forgiveness

How many people do you know who have been in a spiritual situation precisely analogous to my friend Jack's? Fully aware of the sinful impulses that lurk within us, fully aware of the wrongness of an action, fully aware of the penalty we deserve for our sin, we go right out and do it anyway. And then, caught dead to rights, we stand before the judge with no excuse for our actions, no explanation for our stupidity, no hope for release from the punishment that rightly awaits us—and hear the judge whisper to us those incredible words, *You're free.*

How many people like this do you know? I'll guarantee that you know at least one: the person that faces you in the mirror each morning. We have all come to know the tender mercy and forgiveness of our God. When we first came to him and surrendered our lives to him, we poured out before him all the sins, all the uncleanness, all the dirt and filth and slime of our past life—and he forgave us.

Even now, as we continually come to him and confess our sinful words and actions, he looks upon us with mercy and forgives us. "If we confess our sins," John assures us, "he is faithful and just and will forgive us our sins and purify us from all unrighteousness" (1 Jn 1:9).

What about you? Do you still hold in your heart areas of sin that you're afraid to bring to God? The point of the promise made to us in 1 John 1:9 is that we need never fear to confess our sins to God. He is not going to reject us. He is not going to heap condemnation on us. He is going to forgive us! So why hang on to that fear and guilt any longer? Confess your sins to God, who is faithful and just, and he will surely forgive *your* sins and purify *you* from all unrighteousness.

Our Christian walk begins with God's forgiveness and continues day by day in God's forgiveness. We never come to the end of our need for it—and we never come to the end of God's supply of it.

As We Forgive

But God's forgiveness isn't meant to stop with us. He wants it not only to come *to* but also to flow *through* us. Just as he shows mercy and grants forgiveness to us, we are to become a people who show mercy and grant for-giveness to others. We are to be not only a *forgiven* people, but also a *forgiving* people. Our relationships with those around us are to be marked by the same mercy God has shown in his relationship with us.

This is the point of Jesus' parable of the unmerciful servant, recorded in the eighteenth chapter of Matthew's Gospel. Jesus begins with a story that is remarkably similar to my experience with Jack:

The kingdom of heaven is like a king who wanted to settle accounts with his servants. As he began the settlement, a man who owed him ten thousand talents [think of it as ten million dollars] was brought to him. Since he was not able to pay, the master ordered that he and his wife and his children and all that he had be sold to repay the debt.

The servant fell on his knees before him. "Be patient with

me," he begged, "and I will pay back everything." The servant's master took pity on him, canceled the debt and let him go. (Mt 18:23-27)

So far, it's easy to see how this applies to us. Like the servant in the story, we find ourselves needing to settle an impossible account with God: how can we possibly make up for the innumerable ways we have wronged him? And the promise to "pay back everything"—to satisfy the account out of our own resources, our own good deeds—sounds just as feeble and foolish in our mouths as it did in the mouth of the king's servant. We cannot earn our release. Like the servant, our only hope is that the king will take pity on us and cancel our debt.

And he does! How would you feel if you owed someone several

million dollars and they simply said to you, "That's okay. Forget it?" I don't know about you, but I think that would put a little spring back into my step. That's just the experience we have when we receive God's forgiveness.

Now you would think that such an overwhelming experience of mercy would make it easy for us to show mercy to others, wouldn't you? Think again. Unfortunately, all too often our similarity to the servant in the parable extends to his next set of actions as well:

> But when the servant went out, he found one of his fellow servants who owed him a hundred denarii [think of this as about ten dollars]. He grabbed him and began to choke him. "Pay back what you owe me!" he demanded.
>
> His fellow servant fell to his

knees and begged him, "Be patient with me, and I will pay you back."

But he refused. Instead, he went off and had the man thrown into prison until he could pay the debt. (Mt 18:28-30)

Imagine! This guy has just been let off the hook for ten million dollars, and now he's getting huffy about a lousy ten bucks. His master has just poured gallons of mercy on him, and now he can't spare a tin cup's worth for his friend.

That is just the way you and I are when we withhold our forgiveness from others. We have received such unfathomable mercy from one against whom we have done unspeakable wrong. And yet we find it difficult to show mercy to those who wrong us. Instead, we figuratively throw them into prison: the prison of our own pride and resentment. We hold a grudge against them until we decide that their debt to us has been satisfied.

Jesus has some strong words for us about this attitude:

Then the master called the servant in. "You wicked servant," he said, "I canceled all that debt of yours because you begged me to. Shouldn't you have had mercy on your fellow servant just as I had on you?" In anger his master turned him over to the jailers until he should pay back all he owed.

This is how my heavenly Father will treat each of you unless you forgive your brother from your heart. (Mt 18:32-35)

Ouch! It's one thing to point out how selfish and immature we look when we fail to forgive as we have been forgiven. But Jesus goes farther—much farther. He actually says that our own experience of God's forgiveness depends on our willingness to extend that forgiveness to others. We receive only as we give.

Remember the Lord's prayer? "Forgive us our debts, *as we also have forgiven our debtors*" (Mt 6:12). This is just the same lesson in a different form: unless we forgive our brother, our heavenly Father will not forgive us.

That is a very hard saying. Why is Jesus so stern on this point? I think the reason is this: the decision of who to forgive, what to forgive, and when to forgive, is one that belongs to God alone. When we take it upon ourselves to decide whether we will extend forgiveness in a particular situation, we are seizing a function that belongs only to God. We are, in effect, making ourselves God!

Playing God

This was the lesson that Jonah had to learn. Now all of us are familiar with the story of Jonah: how he ran away when God called him to preach repentance to the Ninevites; how he then spent three days in the belly of the great fish as God's way of changing his mind.

I always used to think that Jonah ran away from God's call because he figured the Ninevites—whose reputation for sin and godlessness was rather impressive—would tear him apart if he tried to preach repentance to them. That is, I thought Jonah just had a particularly bad case of the fright that all of us experience when the Lord calls us to speak to others about their sin.

But that doesn't explain Jonah's behavior *after* he finished preaching. A funny thing happened at the end of Jonah's sermon: the Ninevites repented. Far from tearing Jonah limb from limb, they seem eager to respond to his message. "The Ninevites believed God," the account says simply. "They declared a fast, and all of them, from the greatest to the least, put on sackcloth." Even the king of Ninevah repented, and called all the people to a day of fasting (Jon 3:5, 6-9).

You would expect Jonah to be relieved and happy: relieved that the Ninevites didn't do him in, and happy that they had heard God's message and turned from their sin. But in fact his reaction was quite different:

Jonah was greatly displeased and became angry. He prayed to the Lord, "O Lord, is this not what I said when I was still at home? That is why I was so quick to flee to Tarshish. I knew

that you are a gracious and
compassionate God, slow to
anger and abounding in love, a
God who relents from sending
calamity. Now, O Lord, take
away my life, for it is better to
die than to live." (Jon 4:1-3)

Do you see Jonah's problem? He
wasn't afraid that the Ninevites
wouldn't repent, he was afraid
that they *would*! He didn't *want*
the Ninevites to experience God's
mercy, he wanted them to experience God's judgment! That's why
he ran to Tarshish. That's why he
got angry because of the Ninevites'
repentance.

"I knew it," he fumed. "I just
knew it. Those rotten Ninevites.
Getting wiped from the face of the
earth would have been better than
they deserved. But is that what
they get? Oh, no! God has to send
me there to warn them, knowing
full well that they'd listen

to me and repent. Now look at them, sitting there in sackcloth and ashes. I tell you, there's no justice."

You see, Jonah had already made up his own mind about whether or not the Ninevites deserved forgiveness. If it had been up to Jonah, they *would* have been destroyed. But that wasn't Jonah's decision to make. He was putting himself in God's place, making himself God.

God helps Jonah see the error of his thinking in a rather unusual way. As Jonah sits outside the city, God causes a vine to grow up and shade Jonah from the hot sun. Jonah is delighted with the vine. Then God sends a worm to attack and destroy the vine. Jonah, left exposed to the sun and the scorching east wind, is in despair. Again he pleads with God to take his life.

Now comes the punch line.

"Jonah," God says, "let's talk about that vine for a minute. You know, that vine didn't belong to you. You didn't have to lift a finger to plant it or tend it. And yet look how concerned you are about it! Look how its destruction causes you pain!

"The way you feel about that vine," God continues, "is the way I feel about the Ninevites. They may be despicable in your sight, Jonah, but they're precious to me. Whether or not they deserve for-giveness isn't your decision to make. That's up to me. You need to learn to see things from my perspective, and stop trying to do my job."

How easy it is for us to fall into the same trap as Jonah! Our prob-lem isn't that we *can't* forgive others, but that we don't *want* to. They've hurt us, and they need to pay for it. They don't deserve forgiveness—not yet, anyway. We'll let them off the hook when we're good and ready.

But God hasn't authorized us to make those kinds of decisions about others. Rather, he has commanded us to forgive them. We too need to learn to see things from his perspective and to stop trying to do his job. If we don't, we make ourselves out to be God, and place ourselves beyond the reach of *his* forgiveness—a place where we definitely do not want to be!

Again, what about you? Are there people who have wronged you, whom you have refused to forgive? Maybe it's a parent who mistreated you or told you that you'd never amount to anything. Maybe it's a teacher or a relative or a friend who betrayed you or did you harm. Why store up the poison of unforgiveness any longer? Why keep putting yourself under the impossible burden of trying to do God's job? Why keep robbing yourself of the full experience of God's forgiveness in your own life? Call to mind the great mercy God has shown, and continues to show, to you. Then resolve to show that same mercy to the one who has hurt you. "Freely you have received, freely give" (Mt 10:8).

The Prison of Bitterness

The story of Jonah, like that of the unmerciful servant in Jesus' parable, helps us understand the problems that are caused by unforgiveness.

People experience unforgiveness in a variety of ways. Often, in my experience, it is aimed at someone close to them who they feel—rightly or wrongly—has done them harm: parents, siblings, friends.

Sometimes unforgiveness is focused on something that is not personified: the person feels wronged by prejudice or oppression and develops resentment toward "the establishment" or "the government" or towards the members of some other racial, ethnic, or economic group.

I often encounter a religious version of this type of resentment. I regularly travel and minister in both Catholic and Protestant circles, and I am saddened by how often I find people in one group who are hateful and unforgiving toward the other (and it definitely goes both ways). They don't really hate the people who make up the other group, of course. How could they? They don't even know them. What they hate is the stereotype they have developed—a stereotype that is often terribly inaccurate.

This is one of the great tragedies of the church today. We, like Jonah, have come to a place where we hate in a nonreasoning, nonrational way. We hate without dialogue, without clarification, without research. We lock ourselves in prisons of bitterness and resentment—and hinder the work of the Lord—because we won't take steps to understand each other and be reconciled.

The most subtle and damaging type of unforgiveness is the kind that is oriented toward oneself. This is a pattern I have come across countless times in counseling and praying with people. They sin. They hate their sin (and rightly so). But they also come to hate themselves because of their sin, and they find it impossible to forgive themselves. This leads to an internal bitterness and self-loathing that ends up bringing more of the same sin that got the whole process started in the first place!

The idea of "forgiving ourselves" may at first seem a bit strange. I know the reality of it was strange to me the first time I encountered it. I had a friend who seemed to be able to make all kinds of mistakes and missteps, and then to simply forgive himself, shake it off, and move on. He drove me crazy! It just didn't seem fair to me that he should let himself off the hook so easily. Shouldn't he at least feel crummy for a while first?

It was a few years later before I came to realize that my friend had been operating in a healthy way. I found myself in a situation in which I had, quite simply, "blown it in a big way." I had done something wrong, something that had caused a lot of pain and heartache for myself and others. And there was nothing I could do about it. I couldn't retrieve it, retract it, or rehabilitate it. I was miserable. I knew that God forgave me, and I knew that the people I had hurt forgave me, too. It was *I* who wouldn't forgive me.

I finally had to come to grips with the fact that if I was going to move ahead in life, I was just going to have to extend the same mercy to myself that I knew God extended toward me. It was one of the most difficult things I have ever done. But that one experience, more than anything else, has made it possible for me to understand the way people can bind themselves up in self-loathing.

Painful Symptoms

What does unforgiveness do to us? Most obviously, perhaps, it ruins relationships. How can we live in love and harmony with people against whom we hold a grudge? But it also causes other kinds of problems. It can produce a kind of spiritual paralysis that can prevent us from growing to Christian maturity. It can even lead to physical illness.

I remember one woman I counseled who had a major problem with unforgiveness. She had come to me for prayer for healing. She had arthritis and a problem with her digestive tract. As I prayed, I got the distinct impression—both on the natural and supernatural plane—that she was filled with anger. I asked her, "Are you by any chance angry with anyone?"

"*No!*" she snapped back. That gave me a pretty good clue that she actually *was* angry with someone.

I sensed the Lord prompting me to ask, "Are you sure you're not angry at your sister?"

She looked at me in a rather startled way and asked, "How did you know about that?" She then went on to tell me how for years she had struggled with bitterness toward her sister.

In one sense, her anger wasn't

too hard to understand: years before, her sister had stolen her boy-
friend from her and married him.
But that had happened sixteen
years before, and she herself was
now happily married to a man she
loved very much. Even after all
that time, and even though the
particulars of the situation no
longer really mattered, she still
could not forgive her sister.

I told her it was my conviction
that if she did not let go of her bitterness, she was not going to be
healed of her physical problems. I
suggested she write her sister a
letter and tell her that she forgave
her.

A couple of months later I heard
back from her. She was elated. She
had written the letter, she told me,
and then had carried it around
with her for two weeks struggling
about whether to mail it or not.
Interestingly, her arthritis and
digestive problems grew steadily

worse during this time. Finally, when the pain grew so severe that she was desperate for relief, she grabbed the letter and hobbled off to a mailbox at the end of her street. She said that the moment she heard the letter hit the bottom of the mailbox, her pain began to subside. Within three days, all the symptoms of her illnesses had disappeared.

The same kinds of things can happen when we refuse to forgive ourselves. One Sunday after the evening service at our church, I was asked to pray with a young woman who had been in our group for years and whom I had known since she was a teenager.

As I entered the prayer room, I could see that something was wrong. She was sitting in a rather contorted position and had a very depressed look on her face.

"Linda, what's the matter?" I asked her.

"I don't know, Pastor," she replied. "Things just aren't going well. I'm not sleeping well, I can't eat. I feel like I can't even pray. I don't know what it is. I just feel all bound up inside."

As she said that, I sensed the Lord saying the word "unforgiveness" to me. "Linda," I said, "the sense I'm getting from the Lord is that you are indeed bound up inside. You're bound by unforgiveness. Does that ring any bells with you?"

She looked at me in genuine puzzlement. "I don't think so," she said. "I can't think of anyone that I haven't forgiven. I had some problems with my mother in the past, but I've dealt with all that. I really think I'm in the clear."

As we continued to pray I suddenly saw, in my mind's eye, a vision of this young lady thoroughly bound up in what looked like ropes. But as I looked more closely, I could see that it wasn't ropes that held her, but her own arms. They seemed strangely elongated and wrapped all about her body.

Suddenly I understood. "Linda," I said, "the person you're not forgiving is *you*."

Almost instantly she began to sob uncontrollably. We were eventually able to talk things through and found that she was plagued by a perfectionist attitude that had led her to set impossible standards for her performance in various areas of life. This, in turn, had led her to a very unwholesome judgmental attitude toward herself.

That night, Linda was able to forgive herself for falling short of her unrealistic self-imposed standards. The physical symptoms she had shown when I first entered the room disappeared, and she has been free from self-condemnation ever since.

For Jesus' Sake

One of the most touching illustrations of giving and receiving forgiveness is found in the New Testament book of Philemon.

This book is actually a personal letter written by Paul to a man named Philemon. From some scattered remarks in the letter, we gather that Philemon was one of Paul's converts and that he is now involved in pastoral work under Paul's direction. Paul addresses him as a "dear friend and fellow worker" and refers to "the church that meets in your home." There is clearly a prior relationship of love and trust between the two of them.

The letter concerns a slave named Onesimus, who had been in Philemon's service but who had run away. The penalty for a slave who ran from his master was quite severe in those days: often the slave's Achilles tendon was severed, which left him unable to walk and made him a cautionary example to other slaves who might be thinking of running away. Somehow Onesimus has come into contact with Paul and become a Christian. Now Paul is sending Onesimus back to his master, along with a personal appeal to Philemon, urging him to take Onesimus back and not to punish him.

I appeal to you for my son Onesimus, who became my son while I was in chains. . . . I am sending him—who is my very heart—back to you. . . . Perhaps the reason he was separated from you for a little while was that you might have him back for good—no longer as a slave, but better than a slave, as a dear brother. . . . So if you consider me a partner, welcome him as you would welcome me.

If he has done you any wrong or owes you anything, charge it to me. (Phlm 10, 12, 15-16, 17-18)

Notice the intensely personal appeal Paul makes to his friend, to open the way for Onesimus's return. He actually asks Philemon to substitute him for Onesimus. "Don't treat him as who he is," Paul says to Philemon. "Treat him as you would treat me. Instead of seeing Onesimus the runaway slave standing before you, see Paul, your beloved friend and teacher, and act accordingly."

Second, note the interesting comment Paul makes in verse 18: "If he has done you any wrong or owes you anything, *charge it to me*." Had Onesimus stolen money from Philemon? Perhaps. It wouldn't have been an unusual thing for a runaway slave to do. But again, Paul takes the responsibility on himself. "Don't hold him

to account for his wrongdoing,"
Paul says. "Put it on my tab.
Charge it to my account. Act as
though it were I who were
indebted to you, not Onesimus."

Paul has no doubt that
Philemon will respond graciously
to his appeal: "Confident of your
obedience," he concludes, "I write
to you, knowing that you will do
even more than I ask" (Phlm 21).

Do you see how clearly this
situation reflects the dynamics of
God's forgiveness—and of ours?
Imagine this whole situation as a
drama with three characters:
Philemon, the injured party;
Onesimus, the repentant wrong-
doer; and Paul, the intercessor.

Now imagine God the Father in
the role of Philemon, and yourself
in the role of Onesimus. He is your
rightful lord and master. You have
rebelled against him; in fact, you've
been caught in the act. You know
that you deserve to be punished

severely for what you have done, and you naturally are reluctant to face your master.

But then Jesus gets involved. He draws you to himself and brings you to repentance. He says to you, "Don't be afraid to go back to your master. I'll clear the way for you. He's a very good friend of mine. I'll appeal to him on your behalf. I'll ask him to relate to you as he would relate to me and to charge your debts to my account."

What a perfect description of the forgiveness we find in Christ! Jesus substitutes himself for us so that when God looks upon us he sees his beloved son. Jesus pays the penalty for our sins so that all our wrongdoing is charged to *his* account, not to ours.

But this little story also serves as a picture of what *our* forgiveness is to be like. Sometimes it is we who are the offended party and our brother or sister who is the guilty one. Jesus once again intervenes and urges us to grant forgiveness for his sake. He tells us to treat our erring brother or sister as though they were him, and to charge the "debts" they have incurred with us to his account. And as we have seen, he too assumes that he can be "confident of our obedience," that he can count on us "to do even more" than he asks.

You see? You can play either part in this play. In fact, you *do* play both parts in it. You are the sinner who daily receives God's forgiveness because of Christ's intervention. And you are the person who daily receives Christ's petition to forgive your brother for his sake.

Remember the story I told you earlier, about my friend Jack? I like to picture Onesimus as Jack, and Philemon as the judge who heard the case. I see Onesimus standing, dumb with fear, before his master. I see Philemon looking at Paul's letter, then at Onesimus, then back at the letter. After a moment he folds the letter and tucks it away, close to his heart. He leans forward and in a gentle voice says, "Onesimus, you can go. You're free."

May we all have the grace to hear these words as they fall from the lips of our heavenly Father! May we all have the grace to speak them to one another, for Jesus' sake!